DATE DUE	
~~APR 05 2013~~		

The Urbana Free Library

To renew: call 217-367-4057
or go to "*urbanafreelibrary.org*"
and select "Renew/Request Items"

A GRAPHIC HISTORY OF THE CIVIL RIGHTS MOVEMENT

ROSA PARKS
AND THE MONTGOMERY BUS BOYCOTT

BY GARY JEFFREY
ILLUSTRATED BY NICK SPENDER

Gareth Stevens
Publishing

Please visit our website, www.garethstevens.com.
For a free color catalog of all our high-quality books,
call toll free 1-800-542-2595 or fax 1-877-542-2596.

Library of Congress Cataloging-in-Publication Data

Jeffrey, Gary.
Rosa Parks and the Montgomery Bus Boycott / Gary Jeffrey.
  p. cm. — (A graphic history of the civil rights movement)
Includes index.
ISBN 978-1-4339-7500-4 (pbk.)
ISBN 978-1-4339-7501-1 (6-pack)
ISBN 978-1-4339-7499-1 (library binding)
1. Parks, Rosa, 1913-2005. 2. Montgomery Bus Boycott, Montgomery,
Ala., 1955-1956—Juvenile literature. 3. Segregation in transportation—
Alabama—Montgomery—History—20th century—Juvenile literature. 4.
Civil rights movements—Alabama—Montgomery—History—20th century—
Juvenile literature. 5. Montgomery (Ala.)—Race relations—History—20th
century—Juvenile literature. 6. African American women—Alabama—
Montgomery—Biography—Juvenile literature. 7. African American civil
rights workers—Alabama—Montgomery—Biography—Juvenile literature. 8.
Montgomery (Ala.)—Biography—Juvenile literature. I. Title.
F334.M753P38475 2013
323.092—dc23
[B]
                                                2011050607

First Edition

Published in 2013 by
Gareth Stevens Publishing
111 East 14th Street, Suite 349
New York, NY 10003

Designed by David West Books

Photo credits:
P22b, ElvertBarnes

Printed in China

CPSIA compliance information: Batch #DWS12GS: For further information contact Gareth Stevens, New York, New York at 1-800-542-2595.

CONTENTS

Rosa Louise McCauley was born in 1913 into a world divided. Separate public facilities were in place for black people and white people—race mixing was discouraged. Black Americans were treated as second-class citizens.

A colored-only watercooler, Oklahoma, 1939

GROWING UP WITH FEAR

Growing up in Pine Levels, Alabama, McCauley and her family lived in fear of of white supremacists like the Ku Klux Klan. When the Klan was out riding, Rosa's grandfather would sit with a loaded shotgun

across his lap. Her mother, a schoolteacher, urged Rosa to take her studies seriously.

When she was 11, Rosa enrolled in an all-black industrial school in Montgomery where pupils were encouraged to be self-reliant—her first taste of independence.

Segregated facilities at an interstate bus terminal in North Carolina, 1940

Montgomery was the capital of Alabama, and segregation was strictly enforced.

GETTING ACTIVE

In 1932, Rosa married Raymond Parks, a young barber, and moved to Montgomery, taking her mother with her.

Raymond was an active member of the National Association for the Advancement of Colored People (NAACP), which Rosa joined in 1943. After World War II, with many black servicemen returning, the NAACP stepped up its fight against the hated segregation, or Jim Crow, laws.

Rosa Parks in 1956 with a young Martin Luther King Jr. behind her

"JIM CROW" BUSES

By far the worst evil in Montgomery was its segregated buses. A moveable "color line" kept blacks apart from whites, who sat at the front. Even though African Americans made up 70 percent of their trade, the white drivers were often mean and rude to them. Those who protested were often taken to jail.

During the summer of 1955, Rosa Parks took time off from her job as a store seamstress to attend a workshop and learn more about how to be an effective civil rights leader...

The NAACP had been helping African Americans since 1910.

ROSA PARKS AND THE MONTGOMERY BUS BOYCOTT

COURT SQUARE, MONTGOMERY, ALABAMA, THURSDAY, DECEMBER 1, 1955.

IT WAS AFTER 5:30 P.M. WHEN ROSA PARKS BOARDED THE CLEVELAND AVENUE BUS BY THE REAR DOOR AND ARRIVED AT THE FIRST ROW OF SEATS DIRECTLY BEHIND THE COLOR LINE.

FOR COLORED PAT ONLY

Y'ALL BETTER MAKE IT *LIGHT* ON YOURSELVES AND LET ME HAVE *THOSE SEATS!*

HE MEANT THEY SHOULD ALL GET UP. NO AFRICAN AMERICAN WAS ALLOWED TO SIT IN THE SAME *ROW* AS A WHITE.

THREE OF THE PASSENGERS MOVED.

EXCUSE ME...

YOU'RE WELCOME.

PARKS SHIFTED OVER TO THE WINDOW SEAT.

IN COURT, PARKS WAS FINED $14.

WE WISH TO APPEAL.

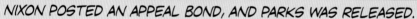

NIXON POSTED AN APPEAL BOND, AND PARKS WAS RELEASED.

IT COULDN'T BE BETTER — THEY'RE PREPARED TO LET THE CASE GO **FEDERAL**.

WE CAN TAKE THIS ALL THE WAY TO THE **SUPREME COURT!**

— IT'S LIKE THEY'RE ACTUALLY HELPING US TO MAKE THIS CASE!

THAT EVENING, KING ADDRESSED AN OVERFLOWING BAPTIST CHURCH IN THE HEART OF MONTGOMERY'S AFRICAN AMERICAN DISTRICT.

HE APPEALED FOR THE NONVIOLENT ACTION TO CONTINUE...

...IF WE PROTEST **COURAGEOUSLY** AND WITH **DIGNITY**... WHEN THE HISTORY BOOKS ARE WRITTEN, SOMEBODY WILL **HAVE TO SAY**...

...THERE LIVED A RACE OF PEOPLE, OF **BLACK PEOPLE**, OF PEOPLE WHO HAD THE **COURAGE** TO STAND UP FOR THEIR **RIGHTS!**

THE 7,000-STRONG CROWD CHEERED IN AGREEMENT.

WHEN RALPH ABERNATHY ASKED FOR A SHOW OF SUPPORT FOR THE BOYCOTT TO CONTINUE, THE WHOLE CHURCH **ROSE AS ONE.**

CARRIED!

THE BOYCOTTERS TOOK TAXIS, ORGANIZED CAR POOLS, OR WALKED. SOME EVEN USED MULES TO GET ABOUT.

LIKE THE BUS COMPANY, CITY SHOPKEEPERS SOON FOUND THEY WERE **LOSING MONEY...**

WHERE ARE ALL OUR CUSTOMERS? WE'RE GOING BROKE!

DON'T WORRY, THEY CAN'T AFFORD TO STAY OFF THE BUSES FOREVER.

The "Miracle of Montgomery"

Under Martin Luther King's leadership, the Montgomery Improvement Association (MIA) kept the bus boycott going for an incredible 381 days. However, it was not the boycott alone that ended transport segregation in Alabama.

Driving for Change

Realizing Parks's appeal would get tied up in the judicial system, the MIA instead went back to some earlier cases where passengers had been jailed under Jim Crow laws. During 1956, they succeeded in getting Alabama district court to rule segregated buses unconstitutional. They kept the boycott going until the city finally changed the system.

The victory of the Montgomery boycott brought Martin Luther King to national attention, boosting the civil rights movement.

Freedom Figure

As the woman who sparked the civil rights movement by refusing to give up her seat on a bus, Rosa Parks became a revered figure who continued to champion civil rights throughout her long life.

Rosa Parks attending a rally in 1998. When she passed away in 2005, her casket was allowed to lie in the Capitol—an honor usually reserved for high-ranking people such as presidents.

GLOSSARY

appeal To request another trial because the first verdict is considered unjust.

bail Money paid to get someone who has been arrested out of jail.

boycott To refuse to buy a product, use a service or attend an event for political reasons.

plaintiff The person who accuses another of a crime in a court case.

predicament A difficult or dangerous situation.

racist Marked by the belief that one race is superior to another.

rallied Gathered together and prepared to act.

revered Honored.

seamstress A person who sews clothing.

supremacists Those who believe that one group of people is better than, or superior to, another.

unconstitutional Against the Constitution, and so unlawful.

unimpeachable Unable to be accused of misconduct.

INDEX

A

Abernathy, Ralph,
    16, 20
appeal, 18

B

Blake, James, 10
boycott, 16–17, 20,
    22

C

Capitol, the, 22
car pools, 20
"color line," 5, 6, 8

D

Durr, Cliff, 14

J

Jim Crow, 5, 15, 22

K

King, Martin
    Luther, Jr., 16,
    19, 22
Ku Klux Klan, 4

M

McCauley, Rosa
    Louise, 4
MIA, 22
mules, 20

N

NAACP, 5, 7
Nixon, E. B., 14–16,
    18

P

Parks, Raymond, 5,
    13–15
Pine Levels,
    Alabama, 4

R

Robinson, Jo Ann,
    16

S

Supreme Court, 18

W

World War II, 5